TEEN LIFE™

FREQUENTLY ASKED QUESTIONS ABOUT

Same-Sex Marriage and
When a Parent Is Gay

Tracy
Brown

ROSEN
PUBLISHING®

New York

Published in 2013 by The Rosen Publishing Group, Inc.
29 East 21st Street,
New York, NY 10010

Library of Congress Cataloging-in-Publication Data

Brown, Tracy.
Frequently asked questions about same-sex marriage and when a parent is gay/Tracy Brown.—1st ed.
    p. cm.—(FAQ:teen life)
Includes bibliographical references and index.
ISBN 978-1-4488-8330-1 (library binding)
1. Same-sex marriage—United States—Juvenile literature.
2. Gay parents—United States—Juvenile literature.
3. Same-sex marriage—Juvenile literature.
4. Gay parents—Juvenile literature. I. Title.
HQ1034.U5B76 2013
306.874086'64—dc23

                                                    2012016550

Manufactured in the United States of America

CPSIA Compliance Information: Batch #W13YA: For further information, contact Rosen Publishing, New York, New York, at 1-800-237-9932

Contents

ARE SAME-SEX COUPLES DIFFERENT FROM OTHER COUPLES?

Have you ever had a crush on a boy or a girl in your class? What made you feel that way about that person? Was it how the person looked, or something he or she was really good at? Was it because you liked how he or she treated other people? What made you feel stronger feelings for that person than for other nice, attractive people you know? It's hard to answer because there is no exact reason why people fall in love or feel attracted to each other. You can't control it—it just happens.

Most people fall in love when they are attracted to someone. It happens when they share interests and when they enjoy being with each other. Many people fall in love when they can see the other person being a part of their life for a long time. That can mean joining their family, sharing a house, growing old together. When

Gay couples fall in love in the same way and for the same reasons as straight couples, and they enjoy doing the same kinds of things together, like shopping.

these feelings grow, many people decide to commit to the person they love. They decide they don't want to be with anyone else. Some couples decide to marry and even to raise children together.

Pretty everyday stuff, right? You see it on television, in movies, and hopefully in your own families and life. It's the most natural, positive thing in the world. But some couples are different—just slightly so—from others in that they are gay and lesbian couples, partners who are both the same gender.

Some people think gay and lesbian couples are very different from heterosexual couples, which are formed by a man and a woman. The word "different" is often used in a way that means something bad. If something is not the same as you are used to, it's easy to think there must be something wrong with it. A new food, for example, may seem weird to you if you have not seen it before, but that does not mean that it is weird. Other people may find it totally normal.

It is often the fear of the unknown that makes people judge others. It makes them label people and assume things about them that are untrue. If you see someone in your school wearing unfamiliar clothes or speaking another language, you may dismiss it as weird just because you don't know or haven't experienced it. In the same way, some people have a hard time accepting gay couples because they don't understand it.

But is it different when a man falls in love with a man, or a woman with a woman, than when a man and woman fall in love? No, it's not. It is as healthy and natural for a man to fall in love with a man and a woman with a woman. Gay couples are not at the core different from other couples. Gay and lesbian people fall in love in the same ways and for the same reasons as any other people.

Comparing Gay and Straight Relationships

How do gay couples compare with other couples? There must be some differences, right? The most obvious difference is that gay couples are formed by partners of the same sex, and heterosexual—or straight—couples are not. But is that such a big deal? Are gay couples different in other ways?

There are lots of stereotypes when it comes to gay and lesbian couples. Stereotypes are general ideas about things that people apply blindly to other people. One stereotype that exists for gay men is that all gay men are sexually promiscuous—wanting many different partners. This makes people think gay men are not interested in long-term, committed relationships. But this is not true. Many gay couples commit to each other and live together just as heterosexual couples do.

There are many long-lasting, stable, and healthy gay and lesbian couples that are good relationship "role models." Perhaps your parents are one example. But even if you are not raised by gay parents or are not gay yourself, there are plenty of famous couples who are very open about their relationships.

Cynthia Nixon, famous for her portrayal of the smart working mother Miranda Hobbes on television's *Sex and the City*,

There are many famous gay and lesbian people who enjoy healthy, long-term relationships with their partners. Actress Cynthia Nixon (*left*) married her partner, Christine Marinoni, in 2012.

recently married her longtime partner, Christine Marinoni. Music legend Elton John has been with his partner, David Furnish, since the early 1990's, and the couple has an adopted son. *Star Trek*'s Mr. Sulu (George Takei) married his partner, Brad Altman, after the couple had already spent twenty-one successful years together.

Lots of scientists have done studies on relationships and sexuality. These studies are filled with facts and figures that can be very boring to read in detail. The results, however, show that many ideas people have about gay couples are false.

Some studies have compared how gay and straight couples do certain things like talk to each other, argue with each other, and make up with each other. One such study by researchers John Gottman and Robert Levenson found that "heterosexual couples may have a great deal to learn from homosexual relationships." The study found that straight couples tend to be more aggressive when they argue with each other.

Gay partners, according to Gottman and Levenson, are less combative, less domineering, and less fearful than heterosexual couples. They found that gay couples use more humor when they argue with their partners, rather than becoming angry.

Of course, this doesn't mean that gay couples are stronger or better than straight couples. The point of this book is not to say that it's better to be in a gay relationship. In fact, other studies have shown that gay relationships end faster than straight relationships.

But science aside, if two people are in love, they generally support each other, respect each other, and value each other's opinions. They make each other feel good about themselves, enjoy the same activities, and in many cases share a home together. When you are around a happy couple, you can tell they are happy by how they treat each other. Gay or straight, it's the same.

Why Do Gay Couples Want to Marry?

Some gay and lesbian couples want to get married. They want this for the same reasons as heterosexual couples—to show commitment and to join together as a family. In this way as in most other ways, gay couples do not differ from heterosexual couples.

For example, comedian and talk-show host Ellen DeGeneres and her partner, actress Portia de Rossi, were married in a very high-profile ceremony at their Beverly Hills, California, home in 2008.

The couple married after gay marriage briefly became legal in California. (Gay marriage was banned again in the state during the November 2008 elections.)

But marriages that took place while gay marriage was legal in California are still valid. For DeGeneres and de Rossi, the difference between being married and not being married is huge. "She's my wife, I get to say that she's my wife and that's just the way it is," said de Rossi in a March 2010 interview on the *Oprah Winfrey Show.*

DeGeneres made it clear that being married was an important step for the couple to have taken. "Anybody who's married knows there is a difference," said DeGeneres in the same interview. "It feels like you're home. There's an anchor, there's a

Comedian and talk-show host Ellen DeGeneres (*left*) married her partner, actress Portia de Rossi, in California in August 2008. The legalization of gay marriage in California was later repealed.

safety. I'm going to be with her until the day I die and I know that." The couple's public statements continue to highlight the sincerity and normality of their marriage.

Showing commitment and celebrating your relationship is one reason to want to marry. There are other reasons, however. Married people have more rights. If, for example, a woman's husband becomes very sick, she has a right to make emergency decisions about his health care. This is not true with couples who are not married.

There are money-related issues, too. If you are married, you file your taxes together. This can save you money. If you are not married, you can't do this. Married partners get Social Security benefits from their husband or wife should their partner die. This is not true if you are unmarried. It doesn't matter how long you have been together.

If a married man and woman divorce, there is legal protection for the person who earns less money. For example, a man might have to pay his ex-wife money every month to help her with her bills. This is not true if you are not married.

Gay and lesbian couples would like to have the same rights as other couples. Marriage is an important right. It means you can commit to each other fully. It also means you have the same legal and financial rights as other couples who choose to marry.

Is Gay Marriage Legal Everywhere?

Gay couples are not able to marry in all states. It is not legal everywhere, but in the last few years many states have decided to change this. At the time of writing, gay marriage is legal in six states: Connecticut, Iowa, Massachusetts (the first state to legalize gay marriage), New Hampshire, New York, and Vermont. In addition, gay marriage is legal in Washington, D.C., and in Oregon's Coquille and Washington State's Suquamish Indian tribes.

If a gay couple lives in a state where it is illegal for them to marry, there are sometimes other options. These include civil unions and domestic partnerships—basically agreements that grant some but not all of the rights married couples enjoy. Many people who are against gay marriage feel that these choices should be enough to make gay couples happy. Others feel it's not fair to allow only some of the same rights to gay couples.

Each state has its own rules about marriage. These laws can change, but that means people need to change their ideas about gay couples marrying.

WHY ARE SOME PEOPLE AGAINST SAME-SEX MARRIAGE?

If two gay people can fall in love in the same way as two straight people, then you may think the next logical step is that the gay couple can marry just like the straight couple. But many people in the United States and around the world think gay couples should not be able to marry. (But rest assured—many people support gay marriage rights, and their numbers are growing!)

It's hard to understand why some people are against gay marriage. If two people fall in love and are happy, why should that bother other people? Why does what other people do affect them, or even interest them?

People who are against gay marriage have no facts to support their arguments. Some people who say gay

Tony B. Conscious (*left*), an opponent of gay marriage, and Daniel Goldma (*right*), who supports the legalization of gay marriage, express their views outside of the California Supreme Court in March 2009.

marriage is wrong don't know a lot of gay people. They don't understand how being gay doesn't make you all that different.

The reasons people give for not supporting gay people or gay marriage vary. They are all, however, a form of prejudice. Prejudice means that you make a judgment about something before you really understand it or have any personal experience with it.

This doesn't mean all people who are against gay marriage are bad people. People oppose gay marriage because they genuinely believe that it is not the best thing for the world we live in. They cite passages of the Bible to support their arguments. They do it because they actually mean well, even though they are wrong. Often they don't understand what it's like to be gay or to grow up with gay parents. They don't understand that they are fighting and fearing something that is not going to harm them.

Changing People's Minds About Gay People and Marriage

If you or your parents, or someone else you know, are gay, you can try to explain to others how it's not that big a deal. You can explain that being gay is just one part of a person. You can focus on how your gay parent or friend is a really good athlete, or has a great sense of humor, or loves dogs. None of us is defined by one thing.

Being gay is not the only thing that makes a person who he or she is, any more than how tall or what race you are tells the full story of who you are. From a distance, it's easy to label people by their most obvious feature. But when people see each other as people, they tend to be more kind about how they judge them.

If you are gay or your parents are gay, you are in a position to help other people understand how being gay doesn't make you that different. You might be able to show them all the things you have in common with everyone else. You might be able to show all the ways that you can be gay and still be a very good person who deserves respect. You can try, and you should. But don't feel discouraged if you can't

Mildred and Richard Loving, a married interracial couple, embrace the day after the Supreme Court ruled in their favor (*Loving v. Virginia*) in 1967. The verdict ended laws and restrictions that prohibited interracial marriage.

change everyone's mind. It's very rare for a person who has always felt one way about something to suddenly feel differently. Change tends to happen slowly and gradually, rather than all at once. So don't expect people to see things your way after one conversation. They may never change their minds.

But laws do eventually change. In the last few years, the issue of whether gay couples should be allowed to marry has gotten a lot of attention. Several states have changed their laws to allow gay marriage. So there are signs that people are changing their ideas about marriage.

There was a time in the United States when interracial marriage was illegal. It took until 1967 for it to be illegal for states to ban people of different races from marrying. This was the result of a lawsuit in the state of Virginia.

But regardless of what the law says, for some, gay marriage and homosexuality itself will always be difficult to accept. And as long as those people don't make you feel bad, and as long as their opinions don't determine your rights, then that's OK.

Homosexuality and Religion

Some people who are against gay marriage feel that way because of their religion. They are taught in their place of worship that homosexuality is a sin and that marriage can only be between a man and a woman. It would be very hard to win an argument with someone who is against gay marriage for religious reasons.

People take their religion very seriously. They won't want to hear that you think what their religion says about gay people is

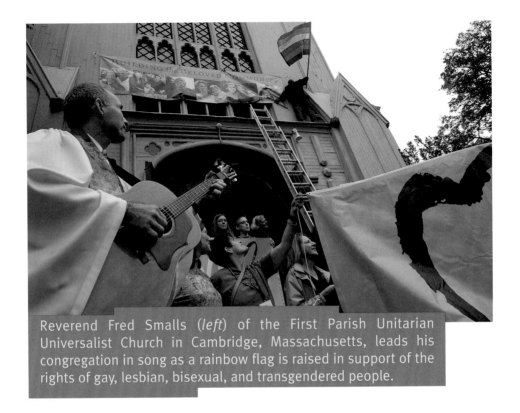

Reverend Fred Smalls (*left*) of the First Parish Unitarian Universalist Church in Cambridge, Massachusetts, leads his congregation in song as a rainbow flag is raised in support of the rights of gay, lesbian, bisexual, and transgendered people.

stupid or wrong. It can be frustrating, but you probably won't be able to convince them otherwise. What you can do is focus on how gay people are still good people and deserve to be treated with the same respect as anyone else.

It's also important to know that being gay, or wanting gay people to have the same rights as others, does not mean that you can't also be religious. There are many churches that accept gay lifestyles. If you want to find a church that accepts and supports your family, you will likely be able to do so. Ask around or look online for churches in your area that are more open and accepting of homosexuality.

How Can I Show People That We're "Normal"?

The number one thing you can do to show others what your life is like is to never be ashamed of it or apologize for it. When you first tell people that you have two dads or two moms, they may think it's weird. They may have never met someone before with such a family. That's OK—and it's OK if they have questions. It's normal to have questions about something you have not experienced before. Just never allow anyone to say bad things about your family. You don't have to accept that.

Invite your friends to meet your family. They will see that your family life is pretty much the same as theirs. You probably have dinner around the same time. You probably talk about the same kinds of things. Maybe you have chores like your friends do and have a similar bedtime. Your day-to-day life is very likely the same as most of your friends.

But don't get discouraged if you can't convince others. That's not your problem. Feel good about yourself and about your family. If other people can't accept that, then there's not a lot you can do about it.

What's a "Normal" Family Anyway?

There are all kinds of families. There are unmarried parents, single parents, married couples who don't have kids, extended families in which grandparents and other family members live together—there are endless possibilities for what makes a family.

Many people think of family as the people they live with, depend on, support, and love. For many Americans and people around the world, a family is formed when a man and a woman marry and have children. It's the traditional idea, the so-called nuclear family. For many, this is the norm.

But in fact, most of us do not grow up in such nuclear families. According to a census conducted in 2000, nuclear families with the original biological parents made up less than 25 percent of American households. And that doesn't even assume that the two parents are married (although it does assume the parents are a man and a woman).

Churches and laws and scientists try to define the term "family," but there really is no single way to explain it. There's no "normal." Your family is made up of the people who love you and who support you. Your family guides you and teaches you. You often eat with them and live with them. Sometimes you are related by blood, but not all the time. Family is much more than a mom, a dad, and their kids.

Defining Marriage on a State and National Level

How people feel individually about what makes a family or a marriage does not impact you. But how the U.S. government and the state you live in define these things does.

In the United States, each state can make its own laws about some issues. Tax and speed limit laws, for example, are made by each state, not by the national government. Marriage laws are decided on the state level, which is why gay couples have varying privileges, rights, and statuses depending on the state in which they live.

Some people are so certain that marriage can only be between a man and a woman that they want the laws to say so. They want there to be a legal definition that protects the idea of marriage as that of a union only a man and woman can form.

Currently, there are thirty-seven states that have legal definitions of marriage. Here are a few examples that limit marriage to a union between a man and a woman:

Arizona: "Marriage between persons of the same sex is void and prohibited."

California: "Only marriage between a man and a woman is valid or recognized in California."

Colorado: "A marriage is valid in this state if: ... it is only between one man and one woman."

Other states and Washington, D.C., have gotten rid of this restriction. In 2009, Washington, D.C, recognized marriages of same-sex couples. In April 2009, the State Supreme Court of Iowa ruled that the state constitution guarantees the right of same-sex couples to marry; the state began issuing marriage licenses to same-sex couples that same month.

In May 2004, the Supreme Judicial Court of Massachusetts ruled that the state's constitution guarantees the right to marry for same-sex couples; the state began issuing marriage licenses to those couples that month.

So although you may sometimes feel like everyone is against gay marriage or that gay families will never be fully accepted, there is reason to believe that the situation is improving. More and more people understand that gay people should be able to be married and have families just like anyone else.

There is also, however, a national—or countrywide—definition of marriage. It claims that the word "marriage" means "only a legal union between one man and one woman as husband and wife," and the word "spouse" refers "only to a person of the opposite sex who is a husband or a wife." This pretty much states that gay couples are not

Marcia Kadish and Tanya McCloskey giddily complete paperwork at Cambridge City Hall, Cambridge, Massachusetts, just before becoming the state's first legally married lesbian couple.

eligible for marriage. But even if the national definition never changes, as more and more states legalize gay marriage it really doesn't matter.

Again, change comes slowly. But it does appear to be coming. The best thing you can do to support gay couples and gay families is to be open about your experiences and your family. Show people that there's nothing that unusual that separates gay people from anyone else. Some people may never understand, but that doesn't mean you shouldn't be proud of your family or that you should accept fewer rights than other people have.

Ten Great Questions to Ask an Expert

1 In what ways are gay couples the same as other couples?

2 Should other people be able to tell you whom you can love?

3 Is it more important to have a mom and a dad or to have a happy, stable family?

4 How can having gay parents help me be a more accepting, open-minded person?

5 Should I feel ashamed if someone makes fun of my family?

6 How does having gay parents make my family life different?

7 In what ways is my family life the same as everyone else's?

8 Why is a gay couple marrying any different from any other couple marrying?

9 How would I feel if someone told me I couldn't have a child?

10 What can I do to better accept and help others accept gay people in my community?

chapter three

CAN SAME-SEX COUPLES BECOME PARENTS?

Given that homosexuals fall in love like anyone else, and that commitment and marriage are important to many gay couples, it follows that some gay couples also want to become parents.

The decision to become parents is a big one. Every couple, gay or straight, has a lot to consider before deciding to start a family. It's an enormous responsibility: raising a child is probably the biggest commitment you can make. All couples have to consider many factors when deciding if they are ready to have a child. They have to think about whether their relationship is stable enough. They have to think about what it will mean financially. They have to decide if both partners will continue to have jobs once they have a child.

Gay and lesbian couples are just as capable of raising healthy, happy children as straight couples, but in some states laws make it very difficult for homosexuals to become parents.

For gay couples, all of these issues apply, but they have to worry about other things that straight couples don't. There are different options to consider, and different hurdles to overcome.

How Gay Couples Can Become Parents

The first complication gay couples face is how they can become parents. It is a matter of biology: having a baby requires a woman's egg to be fertilized by a man's sperm. So what happens when two women or two men want to have a baby? It's a little more complicated than with straight couples.

There are options. A woman can become pregnant using the sperm from a donor, or someone who has donated sperm to a clinic for women who want to become pregnant. This is a solution for many straight women, too, who have trouble becoming pregnant with their partner or who have no partner.

It's slightly more difficult for two men. Men cannot carry and deliver a baby. They need a woman. Some men find what is called a surrogate mother—a woman who is willing to become pregnant and carry a baby for another couple. Again, this is something that some straight couples also choose to do. In this case, the sperm used to fertilize the egg can come from one of the two men who will raise the baby. This way, one is the biological dad.

Options for gay couples are increasing. Advances in fertility science have made many things possible. If both fathers want to be biologically connected to their children, it's possible to fertilize two eggs, each with one man's sperm. The result is twins with the same mom but two different fathers.

Women can both feel connected to their child by one donating the egg. When the egg is fertilized—which means it will grow into a baby—it is then implanted, or placed, into the uterus of the non-egg donor. In this way, one woman donates the egg and the other carries the baby.

There are clinics that help all couples with these and other issues to do with having children. Some help people find a surrogate mother. Others focus on egg donation or sperm donation.

Michael Eidelman (*left*) and his partner, A. J. Vincent, and their twin children, Connor and Katherine, in New York, 2008. The children were conceived via artificial insemination and carried by a surrogate mother.

There are even clinics that focus only on helping gay couples overcome the challenges of becoming parents.

But these techniques were not created only for gay couples. Not only gay couples need help becoming pregnant, and not only the children of gay couples are created through these methods. There's nothing wrong with using what scientists know to help people have children. It is no less natural. Science is a wonderful thing—especially when it helps loving couples reach their dream of having their own baby to love and care for.

In a case where only one parent is the biological parent—meaning the man whose sperm or woman whose egg was used to create the baby—the other partner has no legal status as the child's parent. In these cases, some couples choose for the non-biological parent to adopt the child. Otherwise, only one partner is legally the child's parent. This can be a problem if, worst case, the biological parent dies. The surviving partner would not have a right to keep custody of his or her child.

The Adoption Option

You may think it would be easier for a gay couple to just adopt a child. There are so many children in the United States who need a good, stable home. Why can't a nice gay couple just adopt a baby?

As with laws about who can get married, each state can decide its own laws about adoption. Often, adoption cases are decided in court on a case-by-case basis, so it comes down to a judge's decision.

In some states, the laws do not specifically say that gay couples are not allowed to adopt. In Utah, for example, a single person can adopt, but not a couple that is living together without being married. Because gay people can't marry in Utah, this law prevents them from adopting a baby if they live together. And if you want to have a child with someone, it is very likely that you also want to live together!

In Florida, a 1977 law very clearly made it illegal for gay couples to adopt children. The law was part of a campaign called "Save the Children," the action of people who thought gay couples were not fit to be good parents. Fortunately, this law was tossed out in 2010. Gay couples are no longer banned by law from adopting in Florida.

But even in states where gay adoption is not expressly illegal, it can be difficult for a gay couple to adopt. There is still a lot of prejudice in the adoption system against gay couples. This can mean applications from gay couples are ignored.

According to loveandpride.com—an organization that supports gay couples' rights to adopt—many gay couples are put last on the list of potential adoptive parents by adoption agencies. This can mean gay couples often get the more "difficult" children—children that other couples did not choose to adopt for different reasons, usually behavior related. It can also just mean it takes years for a gay couple to finally be given the chance to adopt a child.

Arguments Against Gay Couples Adopting Children

So why would anyone be against a gay couple parenting? It's for the same reason some people are against gay people and gay marriage: they are afraid because they don't understand.

Rodney Sweigart reads to his son, Bryce, in Columbus, Ohio, in 2005. Bryce was adopted by Sweigart and his partner, Jim Olive, after the couple had been together six years.

The majority of organizations and individual who oppose gay adoption are not gay. They were not raised by gay parents. They probably do not know a lot of gay people or gay couples who have adopted children. They are basing their position on what they believe to be true. Most often, that is that the best thing for a child is to be raised by two parents—a man and a woman.

Some people will tell you that a boy needs a father figure to grow up to be a man. Nobody can really argue that having positive role models of the same gender is not a good thing for any child. But a male child raised by one mother or two mothers—or even a grandmother—can find male role models in other ways. The same goes for a girl who is raised by two fathers or one father. She can find older role models who are women but are not her mother.

Many children—not just children with gay parents—grow up without either a mother or father figure living in their home. A mother can, for the most part, meet her son's emotional and physical needs in the same way as a father. And if such children need something they feel their parent can't provide, they find guidance in other family members, community volunteers, teachers, or parents of friends.

The most important thing is for a child to grow up in a nourishing and loving environment, surrounded by good people who love and support him or her. Many older people in your life can give you advice, teach you about the world, and help you find solutions to your problems. And most of the things that a child really depends on can be provided by a man or a woman.

There are people who believe gay couples are less stable than straight couples. Again, few would argue that growing up with two parents who are in a solid, healthy relationship isn't best for a child. That is the ideal situation. But what makes people think gay couples can't provide the same stability as parents as a straight couple?

There actually are some statistics that show gay couples tend to separate or divorce more often than straight couples. This, of course, does not mean that all gay couples will separate, and to say a couple should not adopt because they might not stay together forever is not a strong argument for denying a child the chance to be adopted into a good home.

And even if a couple breaks up, many children of divorced or separated parents—gay or straight—still have a close relationship with both parents. The chance that a couple may not stay together forever does not mean that they can't be good parents. And the fact that a couple is gay does not mean they will certainly divorce.

Some people believe that being raised by gay parents makes it more likely that a child will be gay. This argument is based on the idea that most children use their parents' relationship as the model for the types of relationships they will have when they grow up.

This is probably true for the behavior children see their parents displaying; children of parents who respect each other will likely seek a mate who shows them respect, for example. But sexual preference—whether you are gay—is not influenced by whether your parents are gay. If that were true, then all straight couples would have only straight children.

But there is also evidence that gay couples are better adoptive parents. Gay people, because of their own experiences with being judged by others, tend to be more open-minded. They are more accepting of people who are different from them. This is a good thing when you are adopting a baby or just being a parent in general.

Most studies show that children who are raised by gay, lesbian, or transgender parents are no different from children raised by straight parents. They are no more likely to be gay themselves. They are just as likely to perform well in school. The important thing for any child is that his or her home be a safe place, and that he or she is loved for and cared for. And there is no reason to believe that a gay couple cannot provide these things just as well as a straight couple.

Is It So Different to Have Gay Parents? Ask Someone Who Knows

Zach Wahls can speak from his own experience. Wahls was raised by two moms in Iowa, a state that recently legalized gay marriage. He tells his story in his book, *My Two Moms*. A video of Wahls speaking at a hearing about whether to legalize gay marriage went viral online. He spoke very clearly and calmly about how normal his childhood had been. He explained that he

was an engineering student at the University of Iowa and an Eagle Scout. He told the people at the hearing, and the millions of people who watched the video online, that his family really isn't so different from any other.

Perhaps the most important thing he said was that you would never know from who he is or what he's done with his life that he was raised

Zach Wahls became a famous face in support of gay marriage rights when he spoke of his experience being raised by two lesbian mothers at the Iowa House Judiciary Committee in 2009.

by two women. "In my nineteen years," he said, "not once have I ever been confronted by an individual who realized independently that I was raised by a gay couple."

Wahls is one of an estimated nine million children raised by gay, lesbian, or transgender couples in the United States. There is no proof that children raised by gay couples struggle more than other children, or grow up differently, or have less stable families. As with gay marriage, people in the United States seem to be more open to the idea of gay parenting. The more kids who come out and talk about how "normal" their home lives are, the more people will see that children raised by gay parents are not in danger. Hopefully people will continue to realize that whether you are gay says nothing about whether you are a fit parent.

Myths and Facts

Children with gay parents are more likely to be gay themselves.

Fact: ➡ Nothing can "make" you gay. A person is born homosexual; it is not something you learn from your parents. Children with gay parents may grow up more accepting of homosexuality because it will not be strange to them. But they are not more likely to be gay.

Gay couples should not be parents because a child needs a mother and a father figure in their home.

Fact: ➡ Although the nuclear family—a mother, a father, and their biological children—is considered the "norm," statistics show that few families actually follow this model. There are all kinds of families—single parents, same-sex parents, extended families, etc. Children grow up and thrive in all environments that are safe and loving.

Civil unions and domestic partnerships are the same as marriage.

Fact: ➡ They are not the same. Civil unions and domestic partnerships do not guarantee the same rights and protection as marriage, and they are not recognized by every state.

HOW CAN I EXPLAIN MY PARENT'S SEXUALITY TO OTHERS?

If you are the only kid you know with gay parents, you may be thinking the differences between your family and other families are enormous. Not because you don't have a great home or fantastic parents, but because other people may think your family life is strange.

It may be hard for you to know how to tell people that you have two moms or two dads. Many people might just assume you have a mom and dad at home. So how do you tell them if that's not the case?

The simplest thing is to keep it simple: just tell it like it is. Remember that you are not admitting anything bad, so there is no reason to feel bad or embarrassed about your family. If you just say, "I have two moms," the conversation probably won't end there, though. Some people may have a lot of questions. Others

Growing up in a family with gay parents is not something you should be afraid to share with your friends. You will find your families have more in common than not.

may not be very nice about it—but don't worry about those people.

Talking about your family is something you will feel more comfortable with the more you do it. So don't try to hide the truth from anyone because you aren't sure how he or she will react. Your teachers and the parents of your school friends probably already know—so be proud of your family and make no apologies for it.

Seek Support from Others in the Same Situation

If you feel like the only person in the world with gay parents, rest assured that you are not. Try to find kids in your area who have similar families to yours. You can look for support groups by searching online. Your parents may be friends with other gay couples who have children.

Of course you don't have to be friends only with other kids of gay parents, but knowing others in a similar situation can have a lot of benefits. You can share ideas about how to deal with people who make judgments about your family. Or you can share the positive sides to your family life.

But you don't have to talk only about having gay parents. That's not the most interesting thing about you after all, right? You can just enjoy being around people without having to wonder if they think your family is strange, and you can talk about something completely other than your gay parents.

If there are no support groups in your area, you can also look online to find kids you can get to know through chat groups or social networking sites. As always when talking with others online, be very careful about the information you share and be sure about whom you are actually talking to.

To that end, there are lots of organizations that provide safe online havens for kids with gay parents to share their experiences. Find one that has a good reputation—your parents or a teacher can help you. On many sites, you can find information on laws that relate to gay marriage and adoption, personal stories from other kids, and resources to help you deal with people who don't understand your family life.

One such organizations is Colage.org, which is based in San Francisco but has chapters all over the country, as well as a Facebook page and e-communities hosted on the organization's main site. The Internet is a wonderful tool for connecting with others who share your experience. But as always, browse wisely!

Don't Isolate Yourself or Your Family

There's nothing worse than feeling alone. You don't want to have a life where you don't have your friends to your house or where you don't want your family coming to school events or community baseball games or piano recitals or whatever activities you care about.

If you feel like people around you aren't going to be accepting, then it can be easy to avoid the problem by just keeping to yourself. But don't. Let your friends get to know your family and experience your family life. And encourage your parents to join in by getting to know other parents of kids in your school or on your sports team and so on. Your parents may be feeling left out, too, if other parents are not accepting of them. Letting people get to know you is the best way to combat prejudice and ease any silly fears they may have. And that can only make your life easier!

If Your Parent Comes Out

If you are born to or adopted by a gay couple, then you have known for a while that your parent or parents are gay. But some homosexual adults, for a variety of personal reasons, do not always live a public gay lifestyle. Some gay adults date and marry members of the opposite sex rather than follow their true selves and be with a same-sex partner. Sometimes they are worried that their families won't accept them as they are if they say they are gay. Sometimes they are not ready themselves to understand the truth. There's no one reason why a gay person lives a straight lifestyle.

Everyone feels better about a situation when he or she finds people in a similar one. If you don't know any other people in your town with gay parents, you can find support groups online.

But if a gay adult has had children with an opposite-sex partner, it can be very confusing for the children to understand when they learn that one of their parents is gay. Any time you learn that your parents are not going to stay together, no matter what the reason, it is a shock, and it can make you feel like the world as you know it has come to an end.

The most important thing to know if this has happened to you is that it doesn't mean your parents love you any less. A parent-child relationship is completely apart from an adult romantic relationship. This is true no matter what the reason for your parents separating.

But learning that one of your parents is gay can be very confusing. It's important to remember that your parent is still for the most part the same person you always knew. It can take a while, but in time everyone is happier when everyone is honest about how they feel. Your parent will be happier not having to pretend he or she is not gay. It's hard, especially when you are still young, but try to support what your parent is doing. It's very brave.

Telling your friends may be hard. Some people will be very surprised, as you probably are. Others may not be so shocked. Hopefully many will be happy and supportive. But remember that your parent is not doing anything wrong.

At the same time, you may feel angry with your parent, and that is also OK. Whatever feelings you have are OK. The important thing is to talk openly and honestly with your parent. Making sure that you still have a good relationship is key. That should be the most important thing. You can let everyone else get used to the news in their own time.

Meeting Your Parent's New Love Interest

If one of your parents has recently told you he or she is gay—which is referred to as "coming out"—it may not be long until your parent starts to date.

It is always hard to see your mom or dad date someone after separating from your other parent. Even when you really want your parent to be happy, it's hard not to want things to go back to how they were. But do your best to keep an open mind and give it time. As long as your parent is making new friends who treat you well and who treat your parent well, everything will be fine.

When you meet your mom's new girlfriend or your dad's new boyfriend, just remember that it's good for your parent to have new friends. It doesn't mean this person will become your new

Be honest with your parents about your feelings, and share your concerns and difficulties with them. They have probably also had to deal with similar feelings and can help you know how to handle them.

mom or dad. He or she might, and that might be a great thing, but you can worry about that later.

Any change takes getting used to. Talking about your worries and your feelings, even the bad feelings, is the best way to make sure that you get through big changes in your family without breaking down important relationships.

HOW CAN I DEAL WITH PEOPLE WHO JUDGE?

There is nothing wrong with being gay. There is no shame in having gay parents. Any child with a strong family unit can be proud of his or her family. It doesn't matter if you are gay or straight.

Whether you have gay parents, have friends with gay parents, or just want to understand the issue of gay marriage and gay parenting, knowing that all people have the right to choose who they love is key.

It would be wonderful if everyone understood that gay couples are not different from straight couples and that being gay is no big deal. But unfortunately, discrimination—having different rules and laws for different people—does still exist for gay people in the United States.

Discrimination is not always obvious. It does not always show up in the form of laws. Sometimes it is just in the way people in your community think and act. For example, if you have a friend who is not allowed to spend the night at your house because you have two dads, that is discrimination.

What can you do when you experience discrimination? The first thing, again, is not to feel bad about yourself or your family. There's nothing you need to change. The problem is that others don't understand how your family life is not that different from theirs just because you have gay parents.

Talk About Your Family Positively

It may be tempting to just never mention your parents. Don't do that. It won't help the problem. Actually, it could even make it seem like you think you have something to be ashamed of, which you don't.

Talk about your family like other kids do. If your dads are picking you up after school, say so. If your moms are coaching your soccer team, focus on how great it is that they are so interested in your activities. There is no reason to hide that your parents are gay. But it is more important to focus on the fact that your parents are your parents—just like any other kid's parents. They do the same kinds of things with you, and your lifestyle is happy and normal.

Some people may ask you questions about your family or home life. It's up to you to decide whether they are really interested or if they are just being nosy. You never have to share anything you are not comfortable sharing. You do not have to explain things to people that kids with straight parents do not have to explain.

Talk to your parents about how they feel when they face discrimination. Ask them what they say when people judge them unfairly. As a family, none of you is alone in how other people treat you. Talk with your parents about how it makes them feel when people assume things about them because they are gay. What do they say? How do they act? They have had years more experience than you with this, and they can be a great source of advice.

Dealing with Bullies

No matter who you are or where you live, bullying is an unfortunate reality that everyone deals with on some level. Bullies are people who like to make others feel bad about themselves. Usually it is because the bullies feel bad about who they are and feel better only when they feel they have power over another person or make someone else feel unhappy.

Bullies will pick on anyone for any reason: because you are small, because you are smart, because your family doesn't have a lot of money. Bullies just look for anything about a person that they can make fun of.

It doesn't really matter what feature of a person is picked on because being bullied isn't really about there being anything wrong with you. If someone bullies you because your parents are gay, it's not because there's anything wrong with being gay. It's because it's something about you that is differ-

Although having gay parents may set you apart from your friends, there are plenty of other things that bring you together. And being different isn't a bad thing—it's what makes people interesting.

ent from some other kids, and bullies are great at finding a difference to make people feel bad about.

You should handle being bullied for having gay parents in the same way you should handle being bullied for anything else: ignore it. Bullies just want you to react to what they are doing. If you don't, they will likely get bored of it and stop.

But if it is making you uncomfortable or goes on too long, talk to you family, talk to your teacher, or find another adult you trust. Nobody should have to put up with being bullied.

And if you see other kids being bullied, for any reason, do what you can to stop it. The more kids stand up for each other against bullying, the less power bullies will have. We all deserve to be treated with respect. What makes us different makes us interesting. It should not make you a target of bullies.

Having Your Own Ideas About Gay Marriage and Parenting

You may live in a state that is very open-minded. Perhaps you go to a school where a lot of kids are gay or have gay parents. Perhaps you have teachers who are gay.

Or you may live in a state that is more conservative, where being gay is not something people talk about too openly. Perhaps you are part of a church that tells you that being gay is wrong.

No matter where you live, you have to create your own ideas of what is right and wrong. They are your ideas, and they count. You will probably hear a lot of opinions about your family or

Unfortunately you will always encounter people who don't understand. Don't let that affect you or your relationship with your parents. It doesn't matter if people object to your parents' relationship—that's not your problem.

families like yours from different sources. In the United States, gay marriage and gay parenting are big topics rights now. You hear it on the television news, read about it online, and maybe even talk about it with your friends.

It's important to value the opinions of others. But it's just as important to value your own. Express yourself clearly and honestly. Let other people share what they think, but don't let anyone try to make you feel bad about who you or your parents are. And don't let anyone tell you how you should feel about your own family.

If other people's ideas start to make you feel angry, try to avoid fighting about it. Agree to disagree. The world is full of people who accept others and don't judge. Focus your time and energy on finding those people—even if they don't share all your opinions. Don't waste time fighting with people who aren't ready to respect you and your family as people with the same rights as anyone else.

adoption A legal process through which an adult becomes the parent of a child that is not his or her biological child.

adoptive parent Someone who because a parent by adopting a child.

biological parent The man whose sperm or the woman whose egg created a child.

civil union A legal contract that couples enter into that has some of the same rights and meanings as a marriage but not all.

coming out A term used to describe when someone tells other people that he or she is gay.

discrimination Different rules for different groups of people, in particular denying some people basic rights.

divorce A legal process that ends a marriage.

gay marriage A marriage between two members of the same gender.

gender Your sex, be it male or female.

heterosexual A person who is attracted to the opposite sex.

homosexual A person who is attracted to the same sex.

lesbian A homosexual woman.

marriage A legal contract that many couples enter into.

prejudice Bad attitudes or ideas about people that are not based on real information or knowledge.

same-sex marriage Gay marriage, or marriage between two members of the same gender.

spouse A person's husband or wife.

surrogate mother A woman who has a baby for another couple.

transgender A person who looks and acts like someone of the opposite sex.

Children of Lesbians and Gays Everywhere (COLAGE)
1550 Bryant Street, Suite 830
San Francisco, CA 94103
(415) 475-9761
Web site: http://www.colage.org
  This organization is for kids with lesbian, gay, bisexual, or
  transgender parents.

Egale Canada
185 Carlton Street
Toronto, ON M5A 2K7
Canada
(416) 964-7887
Web site: http://www.egale.ca
  Egale Canada is a human rights organization advancing
  equality, diversity, education, and justice.

Equal Marriage for Same-Sex Couples
65 Wellesley Street East, Suite 205
Toronto, ON M4Y 1G7
Canada
Web site: http://www.samesexmarriage.ca
  This group works to ensure that same-sex couples have
  the equal right to marry if they choose.

Family Equity Council
41 Winter Street, 4th floor
Boston, MA 02108
(617) 502-8700
Web site: http://www.familyequality.org
   The goal of this organization is to change attitudes and
   policies to ensure all families are respected, loved, and
   celebrated, especially those families with parents who
   are lesbian, gay, bisexual, or transgender.

Human Rights Campaign
1640 Rhode Island Avenue NW
Washington, DC 20036
(202) 628-4160
Web site: http://www.hrc.org
   The Human Righst Campaign works for lesbian, gay,
   bisexual, and transgender rights.

International Gay and Lesbian Human Rights Commission
80 Maiden Lane, Suite 1505
New York, NY 10038
(212) 430-6054
Web site: http://www.iglhrc.org
   This group works for human rights for everyone, everywhere.

Lesbian and Gay Family Building Project
c/o Ferre Institute, Inc.
124 Front Street

Binghamton, NY 13905

(607) 724-4308

Web site: http://www.prideandjoyfamilies.org
This organization is dedicated to helping lesbian, gay, bisexual, and transgender people in New York State build healthy families.

National Center for Bullying Prevention

PACER Center, Inc.

8161 Normandale Boulevard

Bloomington, MN 55437

(888) 248-0822

Web site: http://www.pacer.org/bullying
This organization is dedicated to preventing the bullying of children.

Parents, Families, and Friends of Lesbians and Gays (PFLAG)

PFLAG National Office

1828 L Street NW, Suite 660

Washington, DC 20036

(202) 467-8180

Web site: http://community.pflag.org
PFLAG is a national nonprofit organization with over two hundred thousand members and supporters in the United States.

Web Sites

Due to the changing nature of Internet links, Rosen Publishing has developed an online list of Web sites related to the subject of this book. This site is updated regularly. Please use this link to access the list:

http://www.rosenlinks.com/FAQ/Gay

For Further Reading

Belge, Kathy, and Marke Bieschke. *Queer: The Ultimate LGBT Guide for Teens.* San Francisco, CA: Zest Books, 2011.

Chauncey, George. *Why Marriage: The History Shaping Today's Debate Over Gay Equality.* New York, NY: Basic Books, 2005.

Drew, Naomi. *No Kidding About Bullying: 125 Ready-to-Use Activities to Help Kids Manage Anger, Resolve Conflicts, Build Empathy, and Get Along.* Minneapolis, MN: Free Spirit Publishing, 2010.

Fakhrid-Deen, Tina. *Let's Get This Straight: The Ultimate Handbook for Youth with LGBTQ Parents.* Berkeley, CA: Seal Press, 2010.

Garner, Abigail. *Families Like Mine: Children of Gay Parents Tell It Like It Is.* New York, NY: Harper-Perennial, 2005.

Huegel, Kelly. *GLBTQ: The Survival Guide for Gay, Lesbian, Bisexual, Transgender, and Questioning Teens.* Minneapolis, MN: Free Spirit, 2011.

Pasfield, Scott. *Gay in America.* New York, NY: Welcome Books, 2011.

Polikoff, Nancy. *Beyond (Straight and Gay) Marriage: Valuing All Families Under the Law.* Boston, MA: Beacon Press, 2009.

Priwer, Shana, and Cynthia Phillips. *Gay Parenting: Complete Guide for Same-Sex Families.* Far Hills, NJ: New Horizon Press, 2006.

Sember, Brette McWhorter. *Gay and Lesbian Parenting Choices: From Adoption or Using a Surrogate Mother to Choosing the Perfect Father.* Pompton Plains, NJ: Career Press, 2006.

Wahls, Zach. *My Two Moms: Lessons of Love, Strength, and What Makes a Family.* New York, NY: Gotham, 2012.

Zimbardi-LaMons, Tony. *Forever Dads: A Gay Couple's Journey to Fatherhood.* Austin, TX: Creative House International Press, 2010.

Bibliography

Belkin, Lisa. "Gay and Married with Children." *New York Times*, July 22, 2011. Retrieved February 3, 2012 (http://parenting.blogs.nytimes.com/2011/07/22/gay-and-married-with-children).

Carpenter, Mackenzie. "What Happens to Kids Raised by Gay Parents?" *Pittsburgh Post-Gazette*, June 10, 2007. Retrieved January 15, 2012 (http://www.post-gazette.com/pg/07161/793042-51.stm).

The Colorado Trust. *Bullying Prevention Resource Guide*. April 2008. Retrieved February 2, 2012 (http://www.bullyingprevention.org).

Gottman, John Mordechai, and Robert Wayne Levenson. "Observing Gay, Lesbian, and Heterosexual Relationships." *Journal of Homosexuality*, Vol. 45(1), 2003. Retrieved January 15, 2012 (http://depts.washington.edu/krslab/wp-content/uploads/2010/07/2003-Gottman-et-al-Observing-Gay-Lesbian-and-Heterosexual-Couples-Relationships-Mathematical-Modeling-of-Conflict-Interactin.pdf).

Johnson, Ramen. "Gay Parents: Frequently Asked Questions About Gay Adoption and Parenting." Retrieved January 3, 2012 (http://gaylife.about.com/od/gayparentingadoptio1/a/gay_adoption.htm).

Johnson, Ramon. "How to Support Children with Gay Parents." Retrieved January 4, 2012 (http://gaylife.about.com/od/gayparentingadoptio1/a/gayparent.htm).

Kreisher, Kristen. "Gay Adoption." *Children's Voice*, January 2002. Retrieved January 10, 2012 (http://www.cwla.org/articles/cv0201gayadopt.htm).

Miller, Greg. "Are Gay Relationships Different?" *Time*, January 27, 2008. Retrieved February 4, 2012 (http://www.time.com/time/magazine/article/0,9171,1704660,00.html).

National Association for Research and Therapy of Homosexuality. "Gay Parenting Does Affect Children Differently, Study Finds." Retrieved January 31, 2012 (http://www.narth.com/docs/does.html).

New York Times. "Same-Sex Unions, Civil Unions, and Domestic Partnerships." Times Topics, January 25, 2012. Retrieved January 28, 2012 (http://topics.nytimes.com/top/reference/timestopics/subjects/s/same_sex_marriage/index.html).

Oprah Winfrey Show. "Ellen DeGeneres and Portia de Rossi on Marriage." November 6, 2009. Retrieved January 25, 2012 (http://www.oprah.com/oprahshow/Ellen-DeGeneres-and-Portia-de-Rossis-First-Interview-Together/9).

Patterson, Charlotte J. "Lesbian and Gay Parents and Their Children: Summary of Research Findings." American Psychological Association, 2005. Retrieved January 2012. (http://www.apa.org/pi/lgbt/resources/parenting.aspx

Wahls, Zach. "The Testimony." Zach Wahls Official Web Site. Retrieved February 1, 2012 (http://www.zachwahls.com).

Wald, Deborah. "Gay Adoption Issues." Retrieved February 1, 2012 (http://adoption.about.com/od/gaylesbian/a/gayadoptissues.htm).

WikiHow. "How to Deal with Having Gay Parents." January 28, 2012. Retrieved January 30, 2012 (http://www.wikihow.com/Deal-With-Having-Gay-Parents).

Vestal, Christine. "Gay Marriage Legal in Six States." Stateline.org, June 4, 2009. Retrieved February 1, 2012 (http://www.stateline.org/live/details/story?contentId=347390).

About the Author

Tracy Brown has written several books for young adults on a variety of topics. She lives in the Netherlands with her fiancé and son.

Photo Credits